Lucifer at the Starlite

Also by Kim Addonizio

POETRY
What Is This Thing Called Love
Tell Me
Jimmy & Rita
The Philosopher's Club

FICTION
My Dreams Out in the Street
Little Beauties
In the Box Called Pleasure (stories)

NONFICTION
The Poet's Companion: A Guide to the Pleasures of Writing Poetry
    (with Dorianne Laux)
Ordinary Genius: A Guide for the Poet Within

ANTHOLOGY
Dorothy Parker's Elbow: Tattoos on Writers, Writers on Tattoos
    (coedited with Cheryl Dumesnil)

WORD/MUSIC CD
Swearing, Smoking, Drinking, & Kissing
    (with Susan Browne)

Lucifer at the Starlite

Poems

Kim Addonizio

W. W. Norton & Company

New York   London

For information about permission to reproduce selections from this book,
write to Permissions, W. W. Norton & Company, Inc.,
500 Fifth Avenue, New York, NY 10110

For information about special discounts for bulk purchases, please contact
W. W. Norton Special Sales at specialsales@wwnorton.com or 800-233-4830

Manufacturing by Courier Westford
Book design by JAM Design
Production manager: Anna Oler

Library of Congress Cataloging-in-Publication Data

Addonizio, Kim, date.
Lucifer at the Starlite : poems / Kim Addonizio. — 1st ed.
p. cm.
ISBN 978-0-393-06852-8
I. Title.
PS3551.D3997L83 2009
811'.54—dc22

2009022522

W. W. Norton & Company, Inc.
500 Fifth Avenue, New York, N.Y. 10110
www.wwnorton.com

W. W. Norton & Company Ltd.
Castle House, 75/76 Wells Street, London W1T 3QT

1 2 3 4 5 6 7 8 9 0

For my brother, Gary Addie

Guido mio—you always bring me light.

Contents

8

Each of us must suffer his own demanding ghost.

—Virgil, *The Aeneid*

Io venni in luogo d'ogni luce muto.

—Dante, *Inferno*

Sign Your Name

on a scrap of paper,
crumple or tear it up and throw it away:

that's how the world works, friend.
Maybe you can't even get as far

as gripping a pen, maybe your hand
is scrabbling in a few dirty grains

of rice, or you're licking a tin plate
or just your fly-crawled lips. Welcome

and farewell: you're stacked or stashed
or set aflame, turning on the spit,

the axis, the long pole that runs
through everyone. If you're here

you're already nearly gone. Write
if you can. If you can, give us a song.

I

Happy Hour

November 11

—2004

O everyone's dead and the rain today is marvelous!
I drive to the gym, the streets are slick,
everyone's using their wipers, people are walking
with their shoulders hunched, wearing hoods
or holding up umbrellas, of course, of course,
it's all to be expected—fantastic!
My mother's friend Annie, her funeral's today!
The writer Iris Chang, she just shot herself!
And Arafat, he's dead, too! The doctors refuse
to say what killed him, his wife is fighting
with the Palestinians over his millions, the parking lot
of the gym is filled with muddy puddles!
I run 4.3 mph on the treadmill, and they're dead
in Baghdad and Fallujah, Mosul and Samarra and Latifiya—
Nadia and Surayah, Nahla and Hoda and Noor,
their husbands and cousins and brothers—
dead in their own neighborhoods! Imagine!
Marine Staff Sgt. David G. Ries, 29, Clark, WA.: killed!
Army Spc. Quoc Binh Tran, 26, Mission Viejo, CA: killed,
Army Spc. Bryan L. Freeman, 31, Lumberton, NJ—same deal!
Marine Lance Cpl. Jeffrey Larn, 22, NY, you guessed it!
O I could go on and on, for as long as I live!
In Africa, too, they've been starved and macheted!
The morning paper said the Serbs apologized
for Srebrenica, 7,800 Muslims murdered in 1995,
I know it's old news, but hey, they're still dead!
I almost forgot my neighbor's niece, 16 and puking

in Kaiser Emergency, the cause a big mystery
until the autopsy—toxic shock syndrome,
of all things—I thought that was history, too,
but I guess girls are still dying; who knew! I run
for two miles, my knees hurt, and my shins,
I step off and stretch for a bit, I go back outside
into the rain, it feels chilly and good, it goes on
all day, unending and glorious, falling and filling
the roof gutters, flooding the low-lying roads.

Yes

Do you sometimes drink alone?
Have you ever woken up the next morning
after a night of heavy drinking?
Does your cat wander through the house
meowing inconsolably,
despite having fresh food and water?
Hunger, thirst, friendship, love.
Green Bee, Russian Quaalude, Redheaded Slut:
IEDs on the supply route to pleasure.
There's a gala in your hypothalamus,
helium balloons rising to the rafters,
the fizzy ricochet of laughter.
There's a stumblebum in your cerebellum.
That empty feeling crawling toward you—
should you kill it with a wadded paper towel
or trap it in a jar and shake it out
and send it flying into the grass?
Is your head full of frozen tamales
and a vodka bottle curled on its side?
How do you get through the interminable evenings?
Are they really interminable?
Have you considered the alternative?
Now get out of your car,
stand by the side of the road
and take a step. Now recite
The Waste Land, backwards,
beginning with that sexy Sanskrit word.

For You

For you I undress down to the sheaths of my nerves.
I remove my jewelry and set it on the nightstand,
I unhook my ribs, spread my lungs flat on a chair.
I dissolve like a remedy in water, in wine.
I spill without staining, and leave without stirring the air.
I do it for love. For love, I disappear.

Easeful Death

What a relief to lie down finally,
a No Code behind a curtain,
a hiker slipping off a cliffside trail

or party guest lit like a flambé and pitching forward
off a melting balcony—so many ways
to end, but in the end no one tells you

to butch it up, no one rousts you
from the cozy satin lining of the coffin.
Forget the crematorium,

for there they'll be, your loved ones,
scrounging in the urn for a bit of you
to rub between their fingers.

How much more pleasant to be lowered
into a scraped-clean slot of ground,
the last weirdly shaped piece of your life

tapped into place, the picture completed,
all your longing discarded
and left for the living, like the clothing

your friends will pick through,
keeping the things that fit,
forgetting they used to be yours.

Splendor Hour

> *Nothing can bring back the hour*
> *Of splendour in the grass . . .*
> —WORDSWORTH

Where did you go?
I lost you like that grape jawbreaker
I'd saved for last. I ate
the Raisinets, I ate the Junior Mints
and every night I sat late at the kitchen table
not eating the canned lima beans
or just-thawed peas, until sneaking them
into a napkin or—once—my shoe.
So it wasn't all splendor, my parents
wandering offstage to deliver soliloquies
while my older brother chased the kids with knives
or smacked me with the butt end of a bottle,
inventing synonyms for *stupid* and *ugly*
to apply to the noun of his sister.
It wasn't all cocoons in the apple boughs
and flashing minnows in the creek-trickle
of my self-esteem. But there was something
in the air of you, O hour, if only
because you were fugitive, barely there
even then, glimpsed and soon gone.
Now I think I see you, gleam
of a Diet Mountain Dew can crushed in the weeds.
Cellophane. Pop-top. Glass shard

shaped like lightning. The god
hiding, disguised, so the one
he would love can bear
to open her eyes.

Lucifer at the Starlite

—after George Meredith

Here's my bright idea for life on earth:
better management. The CEO
has lost touch with the details. I'm worth
as much, but I care; I come down here, I show
my face, I'm a real regular. A toast:
To our boys and girls in the war, grinding
through sand, to everybody here, our host
who's mostly mist, like methane rising
from retreating ice shelves. Put me in command.
For every town, we'll have a marching band.
For each thoroughbred, a comfortable stable;
for each worker, a place beneath the table.
For every forward step a stumbling.
A shadow over every starlit thing.

Storm Catechism

The gods are rinsing their just-boiled pasta
in a colander, which is why
it is humid and fitfully raining
down here in the steel sink of mortal life.
Sometimes you can smell the truffle oil
and hear the ambrosia being knocked back,
sometimes you catch a drift
of laughter in that thunder crack: Zeus
knocking over his glass, spilling lightning
into a tree. The tree shears away from itself
and falls on a car, killing a high school girl.
Or maybe it just crashes down
on a few trash cans, and the next day
gets cut up and hauled away by the city.
Either way, hilarity. The gods are infinitely perfect
as is their divine mac and cheese.
Where does macaroni come from? Where does matter?
Why does the cat act autistic when you call her,
then bat around a moth for an hour, watching intently
as it drags its wings over the area rug?
The gods were here first, and they're bigger.
They always were, and always will be
living it up in their father's mansion.
You only crawled from the drain
a few millennia ago,
after inventing legs for yourself

so you could stand, inventing fists
in order to raise them and curse the heavens.
Do the gods see us?
Will the waters be rising soon?
The waters will be rising soon.
Find someone or something to cling to.

The Burning

Dante put the philosophers in Limbo—

Limbo, where the babies who had died
(I learned as a child)

had to live, unbaptized.

Limbo which was actually in hell.

Hell, where the burning was;
the place my brother told my father to go
as they hit each other,

as the kitchen door was kicked in to hang by a hinge.

Hell which meant being far from God.

The babies floating in a white space,
faces stretched like balloons.

God—listening
to me.

As for Satan,
waiting,

encased in ice: I thought

.   .   .

he was in my brother, I thought
he was trying to hurt me

because I was good. The Lord
just hung there, sad example

but Satan kept after me.

Out of love. That's what I see now—
black hunk of ice

in my chest. And my brother,

the family shuns him,
he needs a cane to walk, no job

or friends—he takes our confused mother
to the bank sometimes

and she writes him a check.

He tries to talk her into God; he's religious now.
He says the heart is deceitful.

And I hate him
as I always have

with a great purity of feeling.

There Seems No Way to Get At It

Your mother was a kind of machine,
always dispensing—milk pouring out,

clothing and prattle, then money,
always money, and love—well, the love.

Maybe it's in there, far back;
you can almost see it through the glass.

The scratched glass, the murky glass.
You knock, you kick, you almost scream

the way you did when you were little.
Her eyes close, the way they do

when you visit. She's old now.
Practically immobilized. Talk, threaten,

cry, stand there in defeated silence.
Maybe there's a little package wedged

back in the coils. Maybe the mechanics,
when they open her up, will find it

and come to you and ask you what it is.

Verities

Into every life a little ax must fall.
Every dog has its choke chain.
Every cloud has a shadow.
Better dead than fed.
He who laughs, will not last.
Sticks and stones will break you,
and then the names of things will be changed.
A stitch in time saves no one.
The darkest hour comes.

You

You were a town with one pay phone and someone else was
   using it.

You were an ATM temporarily unable to dispense cash.

You were an outdated link and the server was down.

You were invisible to the naked eye.

You were the two insect parts per million allowed in peanut butter.

You were a car wash that left me as dirty as when I pulled in.

You were twenty rotting bags of rice in the hold of a cargo plane
   sitting on the runway in a drought-riddled country.

You were one job opening for two hundred applicants and you paid
   minimum wage.

You were grateful for my submission but you just couldn't use it.

You weren't a Preferred Provider.

You weren't giving any refunds.

You weren't available for comment.

Your grave wasn't marked so I wandered the cemetery for hours,
   part of the grass, part of the crumbling stones.

II

Jukebox

Where Childhood Went

The teeth sold to the fairies
are tombstones in the graveyard of the fireflies.

By their cold caught light
you can make out the big house submerged

in the backyard creek,
thought-minnows spinning in motes in the attic.

The lovely young parents, so long preserved,
are showing signs of rot;

the kitten named Princess, signs
of invisibility. But look, the old dolls

are doing well; they smile and smile.
And the witch? Darling, the witch was real.

Snow White: The Huntsman's Story

I took out my knife and held her head
back. She closed her eyes. A deer
crossed the clearing, stopped

and turned. I thought
it watched me,
I think it watches me still . . .

I swore an oath:
to follow orders, without mercy
or pleasure. Even the part

you think might have been pleasure—
She wasn't a creamy girl. She wasn't
a girl at all. She was my assignment.

When I took the lung and liver
they were warm. I brought them
bloody in a bag to the queen,

who thanked me and mentioned a medal.
That night I left my quarters,
crouched in the weeds and got sick.

Think what you like:
that I spared her, that she sang
while keeping house for seven little men.

•   •   •

Believe in the apple, the glass coffin
without its covering flag,
where she lay

as perfectly preserved as Eva Peron
until the prince came to carry her away.
Of course he didn't carry her;

the servants did. And when they stumbled
over a tree stump—
if you believe the story—the piece of apple,

caught in her throat, popped out,
a magical Heimlich.
I can see it so clearly now:

she sits up, the prince takes
her soft little hand, and the evil queen
trades her Ferragamos for cast-iron sneakers.

And I remember my place in the story.
I let the girl go
into those fabled woods, in winter,

while the snow fell around us,
white on her black hair,
white on her blue Aryan eyes,

white on her pretty, open mouth.

Dream-Pig

It was following me so I killed it,
I felt kind of bad but it was following me

so I cut off the head with scissors,
the neck was thin and rubbery, easy to sever,

it wasn't a bad pig—more like a dog
that hasn't been trained,

it's not the dog's fault.
Maybe it was lost and needed my help

but I didn't like seeing it every time
I turned around. Are you with me on this one?

Don't waste a thought on that pig.
Never mind how it bled

without making a sound, black welling up
under the scissors. Did I say they were shears?

Never mind the shears.
This is all in my head, all right? Forget it.

It could have been a boy, four, maybe five
years old. It had that trusting look.

•   •   •

Though come to think of it
there was something thievish

in the corners of the eyes.
They were pinking shears,

with saw-toothed blades. I killed it
so it would stop. What did I have

that it could want? This was just a stupid dream
about a pig. Stupid dream. Stupid pig.

Long-Distance

Your wooden leg stood beside the bed
in its tennis shoe & sock, trailing its fasteners,

its amputated man leaning invisibly against the wall.
You pulled back the sheet so I could touch

your stump, the small hole in your left foot.
I touched everything. I was curious. I was eighteen

& ignorant. You told me the little
you thought I could handle.

Thirty years gone since then
to wives, meth, government checks . . .

Last year they took a kidney
& a few inches more of your right thigh.

Your two sons were fed to a different war
& spit back out. Now

they induct the nervous teenagers of Phoenix
into the intricacies of parallel parking,

the number of feet to trail the car ahead.
You & I are a late-night phone call.

•   •   •

You stretch out beside your drained pool,
shirtless in the heat

with a bottle of Jack. I cradle my California wine.
When your new prosthesis topples

to the cement by the lounge chair
I try to hear

what the fallen man says
as you set him upright.

You Were

the bride of gin, bride
of men you followed home & let fuck you

only to discover that they already had a woman,
a woman who would never know

what you had done with her man, never
know what a shit she was married to, you were

enamored of impulse, tearing flower heads from sidewalk squares
that had converted from cement

to soil. How pure your longing
to be anything other than yourself. How difficult

to extricate the stem, only to hold the scattering,
brooding petals

& how you longed for that stem. Little former whore,
self-you-have-almost-outgrown, think

of Clytia, pining for Apollo, her whole face turned
toward an idea of heaven. Think

•   •   •

of the faces turned toward you now, as you recite
from the myth you have made,

all of them listening
to you. Of all flowers: you.

The First Line Is the Deepest

I have been one acquainted with the spatula,
the slotted, scuffed, Teflon-coated spatula

that lifts a solitary hamburger from pan to plate,
acquainted with the vibrator known as the Pocket Rocket

and the dildo that goes by Tex,
and I have gone out, a drunken bitch

in order to ruin
what love I was given,

and also I have measured out
my life in little pills—Zoloft,

Restoril, Celexa,
Xanax.

For I am a poet. It is my job, my duty
to know wherein lies the beauty

of this degraded body,
or maybe

it's the degradation in the beautiful body,
the ugly me

•   •   •

groping back to my desk to piss
on perfection, to lay my kiss

of mortal confusion
upon the mouth of infinite wisdom.

My kiss says razors and pain, my kiss says
America is charged with the madness

of God. Sundays, too,
the soldiers get up early, and put on their fatigues in the blue-

black day. Black milk. Black gold. Texas tea.
Into the valley of Halliburton rides the infantry—

Why does one month have to be the cruelest,
can't they all be equally cruel? I have seen the best

gamers of your generation, joysticking their M1 tanks through
the sewage-filled streets. Whose

world this is I think I know.

Another Day on Earth

—Tsunami, December 26, 2004

Souls were arriving, souls were departing
amid the usual screaming and crying.
A lot of drinks were being tossed back,
a lot of women were thinking about their hair.
People were loving the quiet as snow fell,
burying the cars. More than one man
was thinking about his penis. Birds were landing
on statues, birds were snapping up insects.
Prisoners were tending invisible flowers in their cells.
A lot of televisions were feeling vaguely spiritual.
A lot of shoes were hurting.
A lot of hearts had fallen from the trees
and were skittering along in the wind.
All the oceans suddenly realized
they were one ocean, whereupon
the Akashic angel whose job it is
to record each moment's folding and unfolding
paused, then went on furiously writing.

Forms of Love

I love you but I'm married.

I love you but I wish you had more hair.

I love you more.

I love you more like a friend.

I love your friends more than you.

I love how when we go into a mall and classical muzak is playing, you can always name the composer.

I love you, but one or both of us is/are fictional.

I love you but "I" am an unstable signifier.

I love you saying, "I understand the semiotics of that" when I said, "I had a little personal business to take care of."

I love you as long as you love me back.

I love you in spite of the restraining order.

I love you from the coma you put me in.

I love you more than I've ever loved anyone, except for this one guy.

I love you when you're not getting drunk and stupid.

I love how you get me.

I love your pain, it's so competitive.

I love how emotionally unavailable you are.

I love you like I'm a strange backyard and you're running from the cops, looking for a place to stash your gun.

I love your hair.

I love you but I'm just not that into you.

I love you secretly.

I love how you make me feel like I'm a monastery in the desert.

I love how you defined grace as the little turn the blood in the
   syringe takes when you're shooting heroin, after you pull back
   the plunger slightly to make sure you've hit the vein.
I love your mother, she's the opposite of mine.
I love you and feel a powerful spiritual connection to you, even
   though we've never met.
I love your tacos! I love your stick deodorant!
I love it when you tie me up with ropes using the knots you
   learned in Boy Scouts, and when you do the stoned Dennis
   Hopper rap from *Apocalypse Now*!
I love your extravagant double takes!
I love your mother, even though I'm nearly her age!
I love everything about you except your hair.
If it weren't for that I know I could really, really love you.

Book Burning

On top of all the copies of *Lolita* tossed into a parking lot bonfire
    somewhere in Texas
by Bible lovers—how ironic is that, since *bible* means *book*,
not that anyone who takes the Bible literally is likely to
    appreciate irony—
along with Humbert Humbert aka Mesmer Mesmer and Dolores
    aka Lo aka Lola Haze
cruising through the American landscape in ravishing sentences,
along with Henry Miller and his many lovely whores, not to
    mention
all the delicious meals he cadged off his friends while he was
    broke in Paris,
along with Allen Ginsberg ascending chanting over
FIRST BAPTIST GOD IS LOVE BINGO SUPPER SUNDAY
in a column of pink smoke to the tinkling of little Tibetan bells,
and with a bunch of other excellent books some group of
    spiritually impaired Visigoths
deemed inappropriate and corrupt,

there goes the slim paperback my friend Susan and I
relegated to her fireplace last night after drinking too much
    Sancerre
and saying things like *God I hate this guy's poems*
and *Just a single line of Akhmatova is worth his entire smug and trivial oeuvre*
and *Do you believe this poser got a Guggenheim,* until *rip* she'd torn the
    cover off
tear there went two pages at once *crumple* it all burned pretty
    quickly

until we were standing there gleeful and slightly shocked by
    what we'd done
and now this morning I'm thinking of how the ashes of this guy's
    smarmy imagination
are floating up there in the ether of magnificent expression with
    Nabokov et al.,
and the bastard's probably thinking
that he deserves to have been sacrificed on the pyre of our
    ignorance and ego,
and is right now looking down and laughing, pitying us and
    forgiving us our folly.

The Smallest Town Alive

has one sign:

NOW ENTERING NOW LEAVING

You've passed through & won't
come back. Good-bye,

your life

was so many one-horse stoplights
swaying on wires

in a high wind

a lone dog crossing the street
at an angle

a flurry of porches
you won't remember.

On this one I pose

barefoot in a dress
on the bottom step

an ice chip on my tongue
in my pocket a glowing coal

I am trying to crush
into a name.

Migrations

Over the pond, a shabby group
of undershirts was passing,
barely clearing the barbed wire
of the pasture fence. From a blind
on the far side hunters kept firing

and one or two shirts dropped
fluttering into the sedge and pampas.
Then came the panties and nylons,
skimming the water to see their reflections;
they fell torn and bloodied, clogging the water

and men came to fish them out with long hooked poles.
For a while the sky was clear,
but it was the season, and soon the flyway
was crowded again: above the tree line
baseball caps sailed past, scarves, plaid shorts,

and uniforms—a steady stream as far as the eye could see.
Above them the stiff white shirts
were aligned in a precise V. And higher,
where the clouds would be, the elegant suits
traveled, slow and stately,

though occasionally one spread its sleeves
and circled, then plunged straight down
to ravage the flocks below
making a kind of ragged hole
we all flapped harder to fill in.

III

Dance Floor

Feeling Sexy

There's an arrow wound in my amygdala
leaking honey into my parietal lobe.
It makes me want to say things
disallowed from serious poetry
and employ instead the lexicon of porn spam.
I want to make crude statements involving fluids.
Obscenity, expletive, body part.
Imperative verb, possessive pronoun, body part.
I want push to show up at shove's office.
I want to change my address
to last night's wet dream,
I want a plot in that cemetery.
Come and unearth me anytime.

You with the Crack Running Through You

I can seep in, I can dry clear.

And yes it would still be there.
And no I couldn't hold you forever.

But isn't it drafty at night,

alone in that canyon
with the wind of the mind

dragging its debris—

I wanted to put
my mouth on you

and draw out whatever toxin . . .

—but I understand. There are limits
to love. Here is a flower

that needs no water.
It can grow anywhere,

nourished on nothing.
And yes.

The Matter

Some men carry you to bed with your boots on.

Some men say your name like a verbal tic.

Some men slap on an emotional surcharge for every erotic
encounter.

Some men are slightly mentally ill, and thinking of joining a
gym.

Some men have moved on and can't be seduced, even in the
dream bars where you meet them.

Some men who were younger are now the age you were then.

Some men aren't content with mere breakage, they've got to burn
you to the ground.

Some men you've reduced to ashes are finally dusting themselves
off.

Some men are made of fiberglass.

Some men have deep holes drilled in by a war, you can't fill
them.

Some men are delicate and torn.

Some men will steal your bracelet if you let them spend the
night.

Some men will want to fuck your poems, and instead they will
find you.

Some men will say, "I'd like to see how you look when you
come," and then hail a cab.

Some men are a list of ingredients with no recipe.

Some men never see you.

Some men will blindfold you during sex, then secretly put on
  high heels.
Some men will try on your black fishnet stockings in a hotel in
  Rome, or Saran Wrap you to a bedpost in New Orleans.
Some of these men will be worth trying to keep.
Some men will write obtuse, condescending reviews of your
  work, making you remember these lines by Frank O'Hara:
I cannot possibly think of you / other than you are: the assassin / of my
  orchards.
Some men, let's face it, really are too small.
Some men are too large, but it's not usually a deal breaker.
Some men don't have one at all.
Some men will slap you in a way you'll like.
Some men will want to crawl inside you to die.
Some men never clean up the matter.
Some men hand you their hearts like leaflets,
and some men's hearts seem to circle forever: you catch sight of
  them on clear nights,
bright dots among the stars, and wait for their orbits to decay, for
  them to fall to earth.

Crossing

I stash my heart in my boot.
I've got a broken knife for you.
You're not dying for love,
you're not even injured.
Not a scratch, not a nick,
no throb in the bones,
no slight headache
starting behind the eyes.
I'm walking on a dead ocean
all the fish in my body in free fall.
I adore you sinkingly.
You're what. You're whom.
In every room. A dog starts racketing:
it's you. Siren
ratcheting off the blue.
I tie myself to the table.
I bolt myself to the bed.
When the phone's black call comes
I light another silence in my head.

Weaponry

I used an arrow to kill the spider.
I used a steamroller to flatten the worm.

For the ants I called in an air strike.
Bee that found its way in through the screen:

blowtorch.
The mammals were easier—

a bucket of water for submerging the cat,
a poisoned word thrown to the dog.

For love, only a kitchen match. That
and a stove leaking gas

and waiting until the dinner
was good and burned.

To a Rose

Bone-stick
        partially stripped

I hang you upside down
        with your sisters
                above my mirror—

all drooping heads   all trophies of desire

        O rose thou art past-tense

Even your brother the worm
        has shriveled and gone

        Your silks are best
                like this   unkiss-

able
        and therefore bearable

Suite pour les Amours Perdus

1.

Needle & groove: Chet Baker
whose voice (someone said) was "like being

sweet-talked by the void"   —something else
was playing then, but this song's all

nostalgia, so: blues & night   &
a parked truck in a nearly empty lot (&

three, four, & one)   *I fall*
on your lap, *too easily, for love to ever*

straddling you, face tilted up
bridge & improvise, & then the blank

in the record (*last*):
cease.   Desist.   Lay back and swing.

2.

O too-young, & the perfect musculature
of a dumb statue, but you

were clever. & loved Mahler.
After 19— and his tragedies, his music

became . . .   I forget. Instead,
clean sweat & grapefruit, how you greeted

every dog on the street, puppy,
& how once I knelt, my mouth   fastened

to you, & you moved backwards
slowly   & I followed, on my knees

to Truth—

3.

Bottle rockets out the kitchen window
parchment-cooked fish

dark rum, blindfold, Schubert's "Impromptus"

& the black box that picked up communications
between pilots & the SFO tower—   no one

in this room of memory
but us, dear

one,   & no door
for anyone else to enter, so

in total privacy, we live
in air-

waves, crackling &

                    static.

4.

Ah drunk & stumbling with your
guitar & brilliant   when not

drunk &
or using again, *The only time it's all*

all right   Seeing the nothing
that wasn't there

and then it was. *Adieu, adieu*
Quand il me prend dans ses bras

Il me parle tout bas
Je vois in my dreams

5.

& last but not,
sweet karmic

valentine: The second time
we slowed it down,   and risked

a dirge. Should we have left
ourselves to memory, where we're always

best—   should we have stitched
it back, or let it rest . . .

in love too
and later the singer's

lovely wrecked face reflected
in the lid of the closed piano.

IV

I Am Going to Have
to Take Your Keys

In the Lonely Universe

the moon gets up as usual,
heads for the refrigerator or bathroom,
then lies awake, longing for
the Xanax it resembles.
Sex is a fantasy and a spasm.
Music is a slasher movie,
beauty stalked by horror.
Single notes aren't really single;
they're out on the sidewalks sipping lattes
with their flats and sharps,
their invisible naturals.
That song about Galileo and reincarnation
sends you into hysteria
at warp speed.
So do green Toyota trucks,
each with your ex at the wheel.
You open the box with the new lamp
and the packing explodes
into Styroflakes, clinging all over you.
It's white in the lonely universe.
Also, you have to assemble things
following instructions in a language
that doesn't quite exist.
Please rate the last movie you rented
using our system of stars. Upstairs
the newlyweds vacuum late into the night.

Merrily

Keep bailing, keep bailing,
never mind the rain.
What, no bucket? Use your shoe.
Sandals, eh. You've got two hands, man,
don't whine about the manacles
or the snapped-off mast.
List, list.
Row, row, row.

Malice

Oily, wily.
Whip-tailed.

Fairy-handed, reaching in
to skim the soul's fat.

Rat in the mouth of the man
who calls you *nigger*
as we exit the cab.

Making its nest of shreds in my belly
as I scream back.

Whiskered, feverish.
Or maybe winged, maybe

beaked—ravening over the suffering, glad

for the shiny scraps, gleeful.
Self-lovely thrill

of the higher reaches of air—

then getting beyond even pleasure.
Just doing the necessary

work of creating
(mite-riddled, death-mottled)

the hell down there.

Hansel

We my sister Gretel, oh Gretel left our father's house and scattered and lost did not stop at her old witch woman's cottage candy hungry but kept on into the world, woods. We were set upon by rebels guerillas tribesmen revolutionaries who they raped cut off and stabbed left I my sister *Gretel, Gretel* for dead graves hands, for two days nearly to get we circled back; her cottage, burned ruin, hungry kept us alive. Then Gretel in the night died a creature something dragged her out and half-devoured her it. I filled my pockets I walked I Hansel out recognizing nothing birds circling above me I was a child who liked sweets this is my testimony what I broken know and don't forget everything has to eat.

Sui

Little beautiful abused,
  cinder scrap caught
   in the updraft—

Needle thief,
  She Who Ironed Her Forearm Black,
   bone-bare (healed now—

nearly). Lovely
  girl burning in a glass,
   wick in a lake

that whitens
  opaque, blade-scored.
   Blued and grieving

you keep moving.
  Every time I open
   the box you gave me,

the little ballerina—
  glittering, indifferent,
   the size of a bullet—

unfolds.
  She stands, poised.
   If I turn the key

• • •

she'll turn.
    Trapped on her stage
        with that killing music.

My Heart

That Mississippi chicken shack.
That initial-scarred tabletop,
that tiny little dance floor to the left of the band.
That kiosk at the mall selling caramels and kitsch.
That tollbooth with its white-plastic-gloved worker
handing you your change.
That phone booth with the receiver ripped out.
That dressing room in the fetish boutique,
those curtains and mirrors.
That funhouse, that horror, that soundtrack of screams.
That putti-filled heaven raining gilt from the ceiling.
That haven for truckers, that bottomless cup.
That biome. That wilderness preserve.
That landing strip with no runway lights
where you are aiming your plane,
imagining a voice in the tower,
imagining a tower.

God Ode

Praise having a body to be unhappy in,
suffering the slings and staring unbelieving at the arrows

bristling from your chest as the Indians creep closer.
Praise the oil slick of your loneliness,

the suffocated little shorebirds of your longing.
Here's to the scribbles of alcohol

seeping into the cell walls, the reeling
mitochondria, the deceased brain cells carried out

in coffinettes of sweat. Gratitude, gratitude
to whoever knelt down and shat upon the floor

of the Port-o-Let at the children's playground
where I had to pee last Sunday after pushing my young friend

on the tire swing, after whumping down the curving tube slide
again and again upside down on my back.

Small happiness, followed by nausea—
thank You, thank You! You demented, You disapproving

or possibly AWOL Higher Power.
How high is that anyway? Higher than me

•   •   •

and my grown-up friend doing Ecstasy in the desert,
getting cut up by cactus, floating back to the house

finding water for once more delicious than wine?
Praise You in your aerie, Your maybe-not-there-crag.

Down here on the darkling, fattening plain
we root and toil, and sometimes, mercifully, we spin.

Semper

He says, Here's what men really want: blow job, then fucking, girl on top—or next best, fucking her face down. A fifty-caliber machine gun will take down an aircraft, will damage a tank, and now there's a rifle with a ten-shot magazine, shoulder-fired, for sniping long-distance. My girlfriend quit night-managing the Quik Stop because of all the stress and is looking for something part-time. She'll sneak off to the store and slam down two tall beers so when we go to a party, she can pretend not to be drinking. I put her picture on Dreammates.com and pretended to be her, for a gag. Sometimes late at night I write back to the sad fucks who respond to her profile. I hardly sleep anymore and I still have bad dreams. Being able to sit for hours without moving is what made me a good cop, when I was a cop. My new friend Ray is a cop and lets me ride along once in a while, those are the happiest times I have anymore. When Ray was a sniper in Afghanistan, a pregnant woman got off the bus near the Embassy one day and starting spraying with an AK-47, he got a two-for-one. The kid would have just grown up one day and shot everyone. That's how he looked at it. Do you understand what I'm saying? In Vietnam, a kid came running up with a grenade in his hand, you shot that little body and blew it apart. My girlfriend has orgasms that could peel wallpaper. That's something, anyway, he says.

Half-Blind Elegy

So many little horrors,
so many flashing lights.

One among the many is beheaded.

Hail, the world is with me.
And I am sore afraid.

One is stopped on the road, and made to kneel . . .

Why look.
Because I exist (opening his leathery wings).

I have a fantasy: being tied down on an altar, a great winged
   creature hovering over me. Instead of a tongue it has a second
   cock, it fills me twice, it locks me to itself.

I put on the dress of knowledge, its dark glitter—
I admire myself in the mirror—

One is strung up, one is strung.
That song.

〰 〰 〰

In the evening, in the scattering light, pelicans
fly over the slough

•   •   •

and dive for fish, one eye open

one eye closed. So when they hit the water
the open eye

takes the impact, and eventually goes blind.

And then they use the other eye,
and then they are truly blind, and die.

Is that how the angels dive for souls?

So many memories in the heavens.
So many flinchings here below.

Stay with me, love. Make me calm.

Another breaks the surface and is gone.

Shrine

Our Lady of dejection, goddess of sleeplessness & dread, of owl-
   shriek,
of the old man next door hawking up phlegm, his rasp & spit, his
   heavy sigh,

Our Lady of isolate evenings spent sifting for coins in the
   shipwreck at the bottom of a bottle,
Lady of the perforated heart, of errands looming like the labors
   of Hercules,

Lady of consoling, tormenting memories unstoppered from the
   soul-jar
& spilled shimmering in answer to unanswerable thirst,

I love your downcast eyes, your outstretched hands,
your alcove of fog-light descending from the stratosphere;

I love how you forbear us, how you force our pain to flowering,
unlike God who has forsaken us in favor of those who praise Him,

for I cannot praise Him with my awful strings, with my terrible
   song,
Lady of wind in the yards

tearing down trees in the dark, Lady of sulfurous rain
& washed-out roads & snapped power lines flailing

& sparking, oh my mother, at your lovely feet I lay my bitter
   offering.

In the Evening,

according to the Psalms, we are cut down
and withereth like the grass, so on my birthday
I got up early and put on my suit. *Psst!*
Look at this, it will change your life, the man said,
motioning us toward his store.
A long time ago I was pulled from the place
I cleaned with a soapy washcloth the other day,
bathing her in her narrow bed
by the light of the big-screen TV.
All her underwear was dirty. In the evening
there will be canned chili and Cheez-Its,
there will be falling and femoral fractures.
There will be someone you know
but can't quite remember,
and an underpaid stranger
hoisting you into a wheelchair
you could race down the hall like a chariot,
crashing into your retromingent neighbors.
In the store window was a big dusty bottle
with a schooner inside it
made of bottle caps. Many, many bottle caps.
On my birthday, my mother tried
to navigate to her bathroom.
I took a voyage and tried
to lose sight of the shore

and to ignore the god-sized beings
looking down on me,
their baffled faces,
their troubled expressions of hope.

News

Because no reporters came to my door
wanting to confirm my low opinion
of the Bush administration,

because not even the Jehovah's Witnesses,
who can usually be counted on
to arrive each Saturday

bearing informative articles on Satan's wiles
and the hour of judgment
can be counted on this afternoon,

I have no one to tell
that the load of laundry I managed
to carry to the washer

has been transferred successfully
to the dryer. I even was able
to make myself coffee and toss the cat's toy

onto her carpeted platform
before returning to my bed.
These were little victories

over a sullen god—the one who hunkers down
and rocks back and forth, muttering
that there's no reason to go on

•   •   •

The Little Dog Upstairs That
Never Quits Barking

has suddenly quit. And in the quiet
I wait for him to resume, imagining him
(for I have seen him—his tight white curls,
his anxious, mashed-in face)

staring into space, too sorrowful now
even to cry out, settling
with a sigh in the leopard armchair,
facing the wooden indifference of the door.

Poetry after all is a form of barking.
Yap, yap, yap,
someone please come back.
Take me outside to piddle

among the flower stalks. Cradle me
in the arms of your strange tall species,
grant me a biscuit shaped like a bone.
. . . And now I, too, fall silent. The clock

in the kitchen keeps clicking away
saying *Love me* to the skillet and saucepans,
the wire rack of dishes, cans of soup
and beans, O bowl of sugar, O dispenser of salt.

lifting the stone of today
only to watch it roll down into tomorrow.
And now I feel compelled to report

that when the clothes were dry and warm
I got up and folded them and put them away.
Then I finally dressed, late in the afternoon,

and looked out the window and saw
my neighbor, an old black man who lives alone
and sits on his porch most days

in a ratty kitchen chair. So I got my harmonica
and played a bit of Sonny Terry I'd been working on
and I don't know if he listened, if it lit

a match to the damp cigarette of his joy
I can't say, but maybe it did
in some small and unrecorded way.

Happiness After Grief

feels like such a betrayal: the hurt not denied, not pushed away, but gone entirely for that moment you can't help feeling good in, a moment of sudden, irrational joy over nothing of consequence, really, which makes it all somehow seem even worse. Shouldn't happiness be the result of some grand event, something adequate to counter that aching, gaping chasm that opened when . . . But, no: it's merely this: there goes our little neighbor, running barefoot, no pants, fox stole wrapped around her shoulders.

Acknowledgments

Gratitude to the editors of the following journals in which these poems first appeared: *Agni, American Poetry Review, Atlanta Review, Barrow Street, Fairy Tale Review, Fifth Wednesday, Five Points, Harvard Review, Los Angeles Review, Many Mountains Moving, New Letters, New Ohio Review, The New Republic, Nightsun, Pleiades, Poetry, River Styx, Santa Clara Review, Terminus, Threepenny Review, TriQuarterly, Willow Springs.*

"God Ode" also appeared in *Breathe: 101 Contemporary Odes,* edited by Ryan G. Van Cleave and Chad Prevost, C&R Press.
"Verities" also appeared in *Best American Poetry 2006,* edited by Billy Collins, Scribner.

"For You," "My Heart," "The Matter," *"Suite pour les Amours Perdus,"* and "You" will appear in a limited edition chapbook, *The Late Show,* Underwood Editions.

Thanks to my editor, Jill Bialosky; to Susan Browne and Sharon Dolin for their advice on the manuscript; to my agent, Rob McQuilkin, for everything; and to the Guggenheim Foundation for a grant that supported me during some of the writing of this book.